The Story of BACK to BETHLEHEM

As Told in Luke 2:1-20

(New Revised Standard Version)

In those days a decree went out from Emperor Augustus that all the world should be registered. This was the first registration and was taken while Quirinius was governor of Syria. All went to their own towns to be registered. Joseph also went from the town of Nazareth in Galilee to Judea, to the city of David called Bethlehem, because he was descended from the house and family of David. He went to be registered with Mary, to whom he was engaged and who was expecting a child. While they were there, the time came for her to deliver her child. And she gave birth to her firstborn son and wrapped him in bands of cloth, and laid him in a manger, because there was no place for them in the inn.

In that region there were shepherds living in the fields, keeping watch over their flock by night. Then an angel of the Lord stood before them, and the glory of the Lord shone around them, and they were terrified. But the angel said to them, "Do not be afraid; for see—I am bringing you good news of great joy for all the people: to you is born this day in the city of David a Savior, who is the Messiah, the Lord. This will be a sign for you: you will find a child wrapped in bands of cloth and lying in a manger." And suddenly there was with the angel a multitude of the heavenly host, praising God and saying,

"Glory to God in the highest heaven,
and on earth peace among those whom he favors!"

When the angels had left them and gone into heaven, the shepherds said to one another, "Let us go now to Bethlehem and see this thing that has taken place, which the Lord has made known to us." So they went with haste and found Mary and Joseph, and the child lying in the manger. When they saw this, they made known what had been told them about this child; and all who heard it were amazed at what the shepherds told them. But Mary treasured all these words and pondered them in her heart. The shepherds returned, glorifying and praising God for all they had heard and seen, as it had been told them.

A Musical for Youth Based on the Christmas Story in Luke

by Pamela Chun Wilt and Barbara Day

Setting: The main gathering center in Bethlehem with the inn at its center and a manger behind

Main Characters (in order of appearance):

Justus: A Roman soldier who pronounces Caesar Augustus' decree. Baritone solo.
Mary and Joseph: Female youth and older male (both have solos)
Jesse, Judith, Rachel, Seth, Jacob, Elizabeth:
Travelers to Bethlehem*
Andrew and Sarah: The innkeeper and his wife (both have solos)
Samuel, Martha, Stephen, Rebecca, Claudia, Darius, Benjamin, Gloria:
Local residents of Bethlehem*
Aaron, Alaina, John, Sabrina, David, Lydia, Naomi, James:
Shepherds and shepherdesses*
Female soloist: Sings beginning of "Spread the Word"

*Speaking parts may be combined to accommodate smaller casts. For larger groups, additional nonspeaking parts may be added to the groups of travelers, residents, and shepherds/shepherdesses.

1. Prologue

WORDS and MUSIC: Pamela Chun Wilt
© 1995 Abingdon Press

(Justus *looks up, sees the star.)*

(Joseph *and* **Mary** *enter, they travel two-thirds of the way down the center aisle, then stop.)*

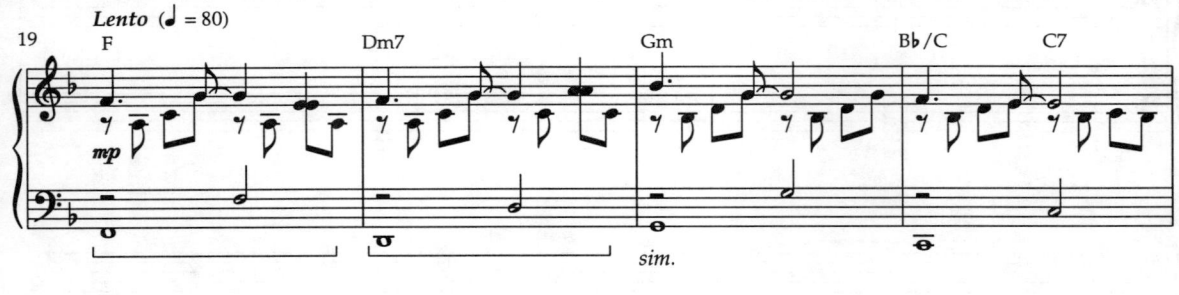

*"Star" motif

(Other travelers enter, moving slowly into positions, then freeze. All are in positions by bar 51.)

*Mary and Joseph look up as the "Star" motif is played.

2. All the World Is Traveling Today!

(Fast-paced mimed action begins. Singers assume characters—shopkeepers, shoppers, travelers, etc.)

WORDS and MUSIC: Pamela Chun Wilt
© 1995 Abingdon Press

*Singers may be divided into equal groups of men and women, or Group I may be all sopranos and altos and Group II all tenors and basses.

(A group of travelers enters, looking for food and rooms. They are carrying bundles, looking lost and tired.)

Jesse: This is unbelievable! So many people, everybody shoving. What a mess!

Judith: There aren't enough rooms. People are camped out everywhere. Didn't anyone plan for these crowds?

Rachel: I can't understand why we can't just register with the government in our town. Why do we have to come all this way?

Jesse: Well, you know we are related to the great king David. It's part of our family heritage.

Rachel: I know. But even King David couldn't find a room in this town.

(Shopkeepers engage in another conversation at another part of the stage area.)

Seth: I *love* this census idea! The people *have* to come back. The money is rolling in.

Jacob: Yeah, but have you seen the trash in the streets and all the animals? What a mess. Next time I'm closing up and leaving town.

Elizabeth: On my way home just now, I passed a young couple in the street. She looks like she could have her baby any minute. I hope they have a place to stay.

Justus: I saw them too. They made me think of my wife and new baby at home in Antioch. I have not yet seen our child.

13

* During second refrain, **Sarah** leads **Mary** and **Joseph** through the crowd to the stable (upstage).

***Andrew** and **Sarah** look up as the "Star" motif is played.

4. Angels in the Sky/Glory to God!

(Shepherds come running in, excited and breathless, as introduction is played. Two or three townspeople wake up, light their lanterns, and observe the commotion.)

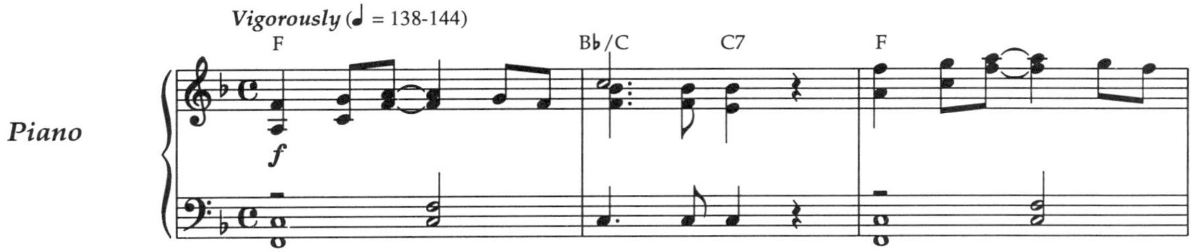

WORDS and MUSIC: Pamela Chun Wilt
© 1995 Abingdon Press

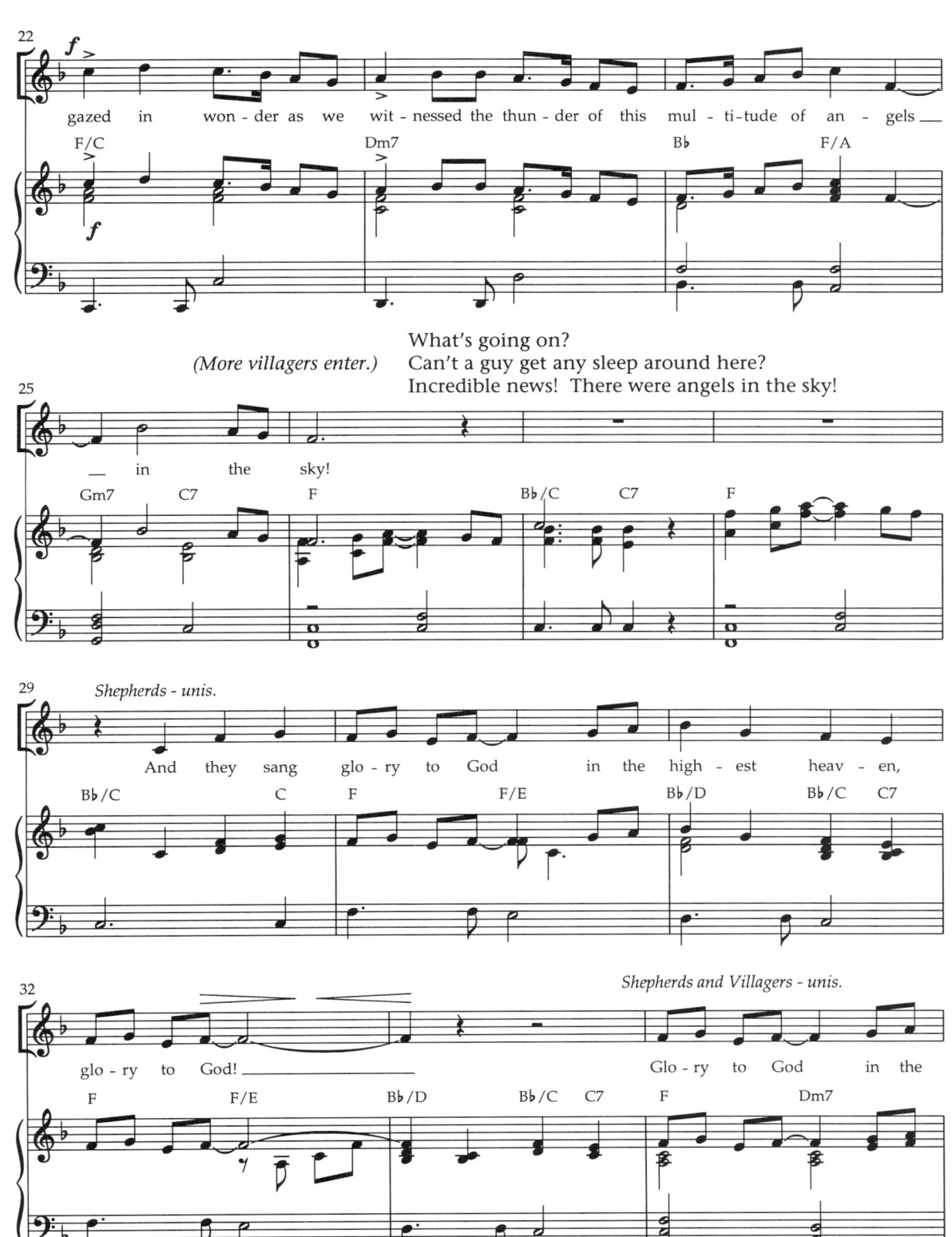

60
Optional Women's Descant
Peace on
an - gel of God in a voice so clear gave them joy - ous news to shout,
Glo - ry to God! And on earth be
F Em7 G/A A7 D
63
mp
earth a Sav - ior born! Then
dolce
joy - ous news a - bout a babe a Sav - ior born! Then
peace, be peace a - mong those whom he fa - vors.
Gm C7 F sus F

*Shepherds move through the crowd to the manger. Dialogue begins immediately after music finishes.
(In four groups at different locations on the stage.)

Group 1
- **Samuel:** I'm glad I'm gettin' out of here soon.
- **Martha:** Those country folk are a little strange. Angels! they said.

Group 2
- **Stephen:** I don't know: I thought I heard something. Did you hear it, Rebecca?
- **Rebecca:** What I hear now is a lot of noise down there. Let's go see what's happening.

Group 3
- **Claudia:** They said it was down by Andrew's place—down below where he keeps his animals.
- **Darius:** Let's go.

Group 4
- **Benjamin:** Just last night I was saying how nothing ever happens in this little town—same routine over and over.
- **Gloria:** Wonder how they found Andrew's place. It's way down this alley. *(Shouting)* Hey, Andy, we hear you've got some excitement out back.

- **Andrew:** *(In front of the inn)* You know, it's the strangest thing. They came to my door looking for shelter—and they were sure going to need it—her about to have that baby and all—but even as I showed them the spot, down below by the animals, they were so calm, not worried at all. *(Musing)* I can't quite figure it. They have a peace about them. Well, anyway, they are a nice couple. And now here come these shepherds out of the fields talking about angels and songs from heaven. It's a strange one, all right.
- **Gloria:** Could we see the baby, do you think?
- **Sarah:** Sure, come on back. Half the town is already there.

*(A space opens up to reveal **Mary** and **Joseph** and the manger—the only "traditional" piece of the set. People move first in curiosity, then a bit of awe as **Mary** begins singing.)*

5. Peace to You

*During verse 3 (instrumental), **Aaron** and **Alaina** move downstage and speak the dialogue on page 27.
**Optional flute, recorder, or keyboard may play melody during instrumental verse.
WORDS and MUSIC: Pamela Chun Wilt
© 1995 Abingdon Press

Dialogue during verse 3 (instrumental)

Aaron: You just never know when something really unusual will happen.
Alaina: What's so unusual about a baby?
Aaron: Well, I mean, you have babies born all the time that's true, but all this angel business. What about that?
Alaina: You're right. That *is* unusual. What do you suppose it means?

(Shepherds move downstage, away from the stable area.)

John: Did you see that? Wow . . . that little baby just lying there!

Sabrina: And did you hear what the mother said about peace—and being foretold by **prophets**?

David: And all those people!

Lydia: *(Looking up)* Sure is bright out tonight. I've never seen the stars like this.

Naomi: I've been watching this town from over in that pasture every night for fifteen years, and there's never been a brightness like this.

James: Guess we'd better head on home.

Sabrina: Wonder if those angels will appear again?

John: Think we could come back and see the baby?

Naomi: I still don't get it. We have been going along these hills all our lives and **nothing** like this before. . . .

David: It's lucky you weren't asleep like you are most nights!

Lydia: Well, I don't really understand it but I believe we did see and hear the angels and we saw the baby and it was peaceful all around. I praise God for what has happened to us.

Naomi: Let's go. I can't wait to tell Ruben and Zack and the others!

6. Spread the Word

WORDS and MUSIC: Pamela Chun Wilt
© 1995 Abingdon Press

20
Soprano
Alto
Ev - 'ry - one,
Men
F F sus F F sus F F sus
23
Ev - 'ry - one, praise the Ho - ly Child,
praise the Ho - ly Child, pon - der, won - der, un - der - stand.
Ev - 'ry - one, praise the Ho - ly Child, pon - der, won - der,
F F sus F F sus F F sus

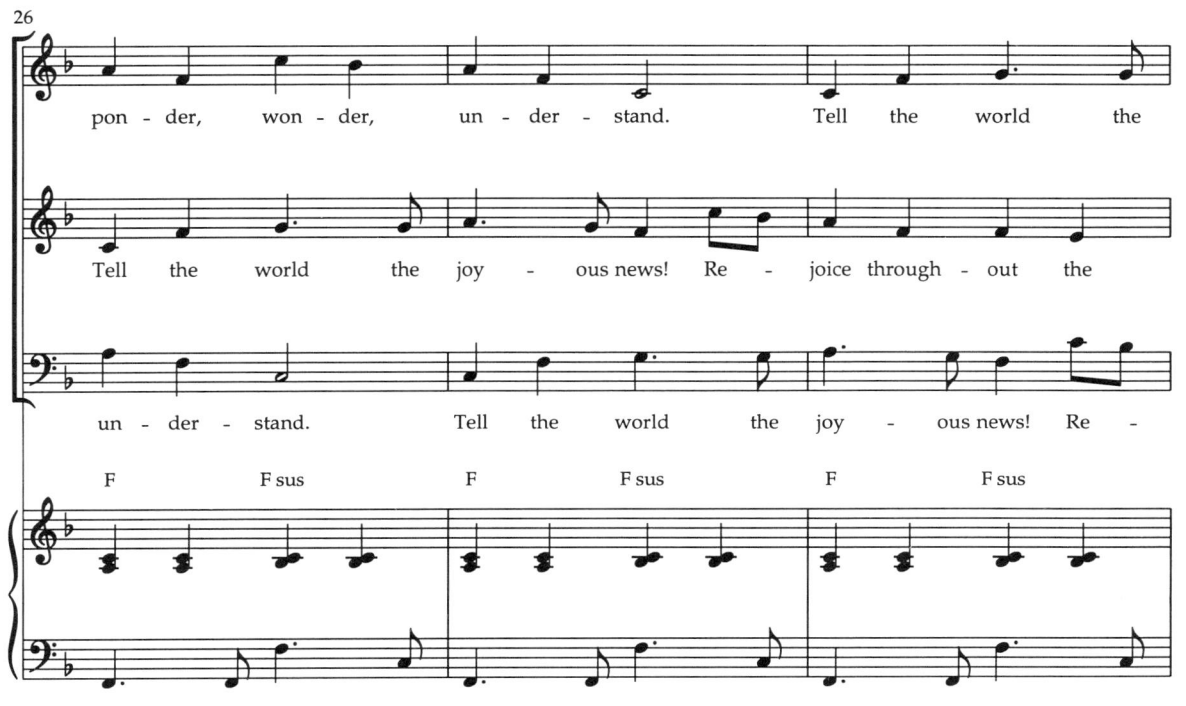

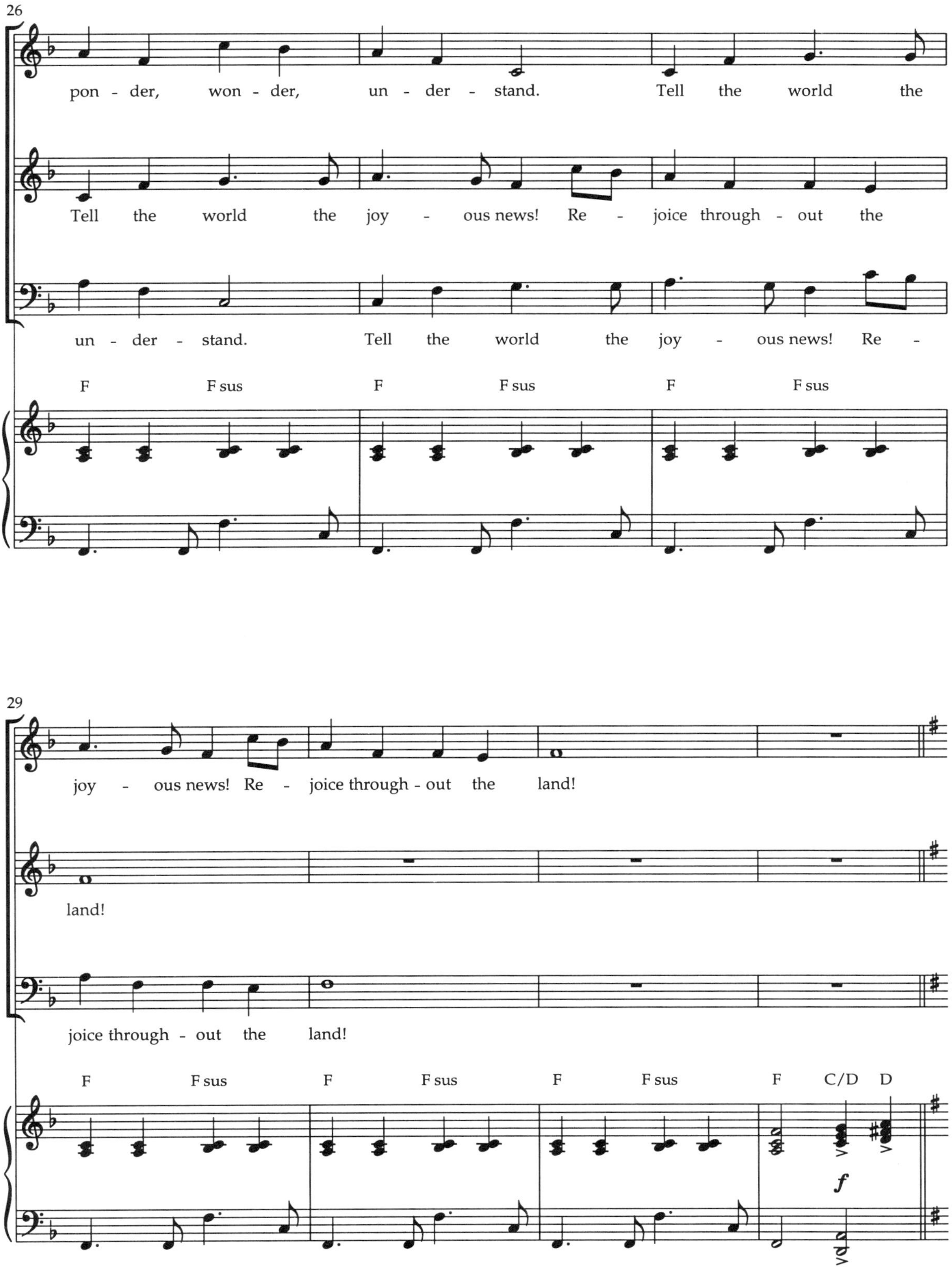
26
pon - der, won - der, un - der - stand. Tell the world the
Tell the world the joy - ous news! Re - joice through - out the
un - der - stand. Tell the world the joy - ous news! Re -
F F sus F F sus F F sus
29
joy - ous news! Re - joice through - out the land!
land!
joice through - out the land!
F F sus F F sus F F sus F C/D D
f

(Shepherds leave, spreading the news [in pantomime] to those gathered as they go.)

Jesse: This town will never be the same.

Judith: It was so unexpected.

Rachel: The word *peace* just keeps going through my mind. You know, it was peaceful—and yet it was exciting.

Seth: And did you notice—all those people who had been arguing and shouting and hurrying were just changed when they saw that baby.

Rachel: Pretty amazing!

Jacob: Anybody seen the shepherds today? They are the ones who saw it first. We were all asleep, but they were watching.

Judith: I think I'll start watching now—just trying to see some new things.

Seth: One thing is for sure. I thought going back to Bethlehem would just be the same old boring time, a lot of hassle. But who would have imagined—a baby?

Jesse: With angels!

All: In Bethlehem!

7. All the World Is Traveling Today!
(Reprise)

(Shepherds "travel" back to stage during introduction.)

*Singers may be divided into equal groups of men and women, or Group I may be all sopranos and altos and Group II all tenors and basses.

WORDS and MUSIC: Pamela Chun Wilt
© 1995 Abingdon Press

8. Peace to You
(Reprise)

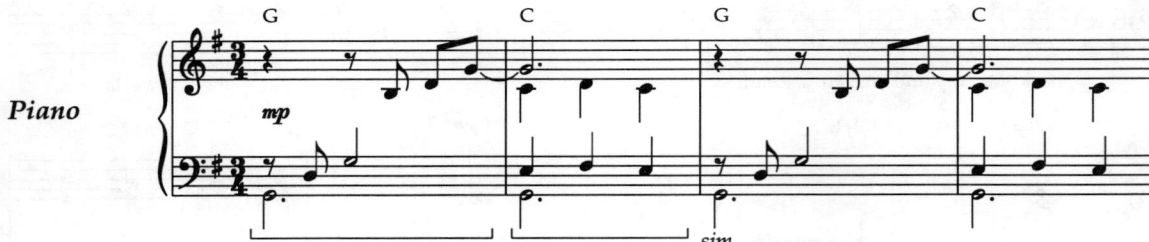

WORDS and MUSIC: Pamela Chun Wilt
© 1995 Abingdon Press

*(All look up at the star.)

9. Exit Music

Repeat 7 as instrumental.

Back to Bethlehem

Containing music that is easy and fun to learn, *Back to Bethlehem* allows youth grades 6-12 to learn music and the Bible story. Based on Luke 2:1-20, this thirty-minute musical portrays the theme of traveling the Christmas journey through a series of songs that advance the story dramatized in the intervening scenes. Accessible to choirs of any size and ability level, the musical is easily staged and produced.

The *Singer's Edition* contains all the music and narration of *Back to Bethlehem*. Also available is a *Leader/Accompanist Edition* that contains easy-to-follow production notes, script, music, step-by-step session plans, and reproducible pages of instruction.

Pamela Chun Wilt (composer) has most recently served at First United Methodist Church in Westfield, New Jersey, and has published music with Abingdon Press in *Church Music Workshop* and *Church Music for Children*.

Barbara Day (session plan writer) is a diaconal minister of music of the North Georgia Conference of The United Methodist Church. She holds a Master's degree in theology and certification in church music.

Also available:
Leader/Accompanist Edition
Listening Tape
Accompaniment Tape

Abingdon Press

ISBN 0-687-01077-2